What Breathes Us

Santa Barbara Poets Laureate

2005–2015

Also from Gunpowder Press:
The Tarnation of Faust: Poems by David Case
Mouth & Fruit: Poems by Chryss Yost
Shaping Water: Poems by Barry Spacks
Original Face: Poems by Jim Peterson
Instead of Sadness: Poems by Catherine Abbey Hodges

Shoreline Voices Projects:
Buzz: Poets Respond to SWARM
Rare Feathers: Poems on Birds & Art

What Breathes Us

Santa Barbara Poets Laureate

2005–2015

Edited by
David Starkey

Gunpowder Press • Santa Barbara
2016

© 2016 David Starkey

Published by Gunpowder Press
David Starkey, Editor
PO Box 60035
Santa Barbara, CA 93160-0035

Front Cover: "R Beach Memory" by Chris Potter
Barry Spacks photo: Mark Robert Halper
Perie Longo photo: R.S. Thurston Photography
David Starkey photo: Stacey J. Byers
Paul J. Willis photo: Brad Elliott
Chryss Yost photo: George Yatchisin
Sojourner Kincaid Rolle photo: Rod Rolle

ISBN-13: 978-0-9916651-8-1

www.gunpowderpress.com

Made possible with support and funding from
The City of Santa Barbara,
Santa Barbara Beautiful
and the
Santa Barbara County Arts Commission.

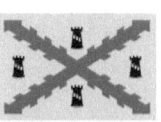

Mayor Helene Schneider

Preface

Words matter.

In public discourse, inside City Hall, during public comment, and from the dais: speech leads to dialogue towards decisions that affect our everyday lives. What is said, and how it is said, matters as it shapes our views and hopefully creates consensus and progressive social change. It is the method of how things get done—how government works.

Poetry, especially when recited out loud, has the incredible quality of perfectly capturing a moment, or a picture, or a thought, or a fleeting notion. In our multifaceted world with competing interests and constant distractions, I find it both soothing and energizing when people gather together and listen to a poem, especially when presented by the poet who created the piece for that specific occasion.

Santa Barbara has a long history of celebrating poetry, and poets. At the turn of the last millennium, members of our artistic community created an unofficial Poet Laureate position to celebrate the written word and crowned David Oliveira with the laurel wreath. A few years later, I as a Santa Barbara City Councilmember and liaison to the City Arts Advisory Committee, along with Mayor Marty Blum, initiated a proposal to create an official Poet Laureate position that would serve at the behest of the City of Santa Barbara for a two-year team. The Santa Barbara City Council passed a resolution creating the position in 2004 and Barry Spacks was proclaimed as the City's first Poet Laureate in April 2005, in time to celebrate National Poetry Month.

This past decade, our community has benefitted from six creative and civically engaged residents who have officially served as the City of Santa Barbara's Poets Laureate: Barry Spacks, Perie Longo, David Starkey, Paul Willis, Chryss Yost and Sojourner Kincaid Rolle. Each of them have played an important role setting the tone at various official ceremonies: Swearing-in of new Councilmembers and Mayors, Proclaiming National

Poetry Month, even Ribbon Cutting ceremonies at seemingly random places like a new affordable housing development, a remodeled children's library and a water treatment plant. They connect with multiple community-based organizations and local businesses, and they infuse a new excitement about the spoken word and the art of poetry with students and seniors alike. Their work polishes Santa Barbara's creative economic engine, allowing us all to dream big and act accordingly. They all have help connect the dots between City Hall and our greater community.

It is truly an honor as Mayor to officially thank them for their service and recognize their words and deeds here.

Celebrating words:
Santa Barbarans value our
Poets Laureate

—Mayor Helene Schneider

Contents

Barry Spacks

Spacks Street	17
What Breathes Us	18
The Hope of the Air	19
Within Another Life	20
An Emblem of Two Foxes (Spacks Street)	21
Whitewater Vision	22
At 35	23
Buddha Songs	24
The Cow	25

Perie Longo

Student Poetry Recitation: Santa Barbara Courthouse Mural Room	29
The Way of Santa Barbara	31
"What Do Women Want?"	33
The Age When Anything Is Possible	35
Thirst: Kuwait Poetry Workshop	37
What We Live For...	38
Dedication	39
The Veil	40
Something Small	41

David Starkey

The Difference Between Poets and Politicians	45
Lawnmower	46
Spring Flowers	48

A Few Things You Should Know about the Finns	50
What the Sea Can Hold	51
In Praise of the Public Library	52
Bibliothèque du Soleil	54
Nuns in Rome	55
Fire-following Flowers	56

PAUL J. WILLIS

Just after Groundhog Day	61
A Story of Hands	62
Midsummer	63
Extra Innings	64
Intercession	65
On City Council	66
What We Have	67
Refugio	68
On the 225th Year of Mission Santa Barbara	69

CHRYSS YOST

Eduardo Recites Keats' "Ode on a Grecian Urn"	75
The Flow	76
California Roots	77
Furious Bread	78
Naked Ladies at the End of Summer	79
Portrait of a Saint with Schwinn and BBQ Sauce	80
Wicked	82
Lai with Sounds of Skin	83
Last Night	84

SOJOURNER KINCAID ROLLE

A Song of Santa Barbara	89
A Space Where a Poem Ought to Be	92
Circle of Painted Stones	94
Hosanna	96
Inseparable	98
A Charge To Keep In Mind	100
An Ode to the King Palm at Anacapa Street	102
Where The Hum Begins	103

CODA: DAVID OLIVEIRA, MILLENNIUM POET LAUREATE

The End of the Twentieth Century	109

2005–2007

Barry Spacks

Barry Spacks

The choice of Barry Spacks as Santa Barbara's first official Poet Laureate in 2005 was met with universal approval by the community. For decades, Spacks had been central to the Santa Barbara poetry scene, not just as a professor at the University of California-Santa Barbara, but also as a friend and mentor to many of the city's poets. He was generous with his praise and encouragement but also fierce in his beliefs about poetry. Friend and fellow poet John Ridland observed, "his was a creative, not a destructive, talent, whether in his own work or helping others with theirs."

Spacks was famous for attending poetry events around the city, both large and small, where he always made a distinct impression. Poet Teddy Macker remembers his first class at UCSB with his future mentor:

> Barry didn't look like the other professors. There was a wildness to him, something that told you he was intimate with the elements. He had long, frazzled salt-and-pepper hair—hair he wore in a ponytail—and a little gold earring. He sometimes wore a T-shirt that said ENLIGHTENED MIND. He sometimes wore a big sunhat. There was some turquoise in his wedding ring. And he had a beard like Poseidon.

Barry Spacks was born in Philadelphia in 1931. He taught at MIT from 1960 to 1981, then at the University of California-Santa Barbara, for 32 years. A recipient of the St. Botolph's Arts Award, he published eleven poetry collections during his lifetime, including *Spacks Street: New and Selected Poems* (Johns Hopkins University Press, 1982), which won the Commonwealth Club of California's Poetry Medal. A practitioner of Tibetan Buddhism with his wife Kimberley Snow, Spacks's work was suffused with a wisdom, tranquility, kindness and playfulness he often attributed to Buddhism.

Although not as widely anthologized as some of his American peers, Spacks nevertheless had a devoted following around the country, especially among other poets, who appreciated his gift for wit and aphorism and his inimitable ear for the music of poetry. Former United States Poet Laureate Robert Pinsky praised the "omnivorous, generous quality in Barry Spacks' late poems, as in Barry's presence." Fiction writer Tobias Wolff said that he had "loved the poetry of Barry Spacks ever since I began reading him some forty years ago—to the point of taping poems of his above my desk. You sense in every one of them the presence of a particular spirit—a spirit of great humor and great seriousness, honesty and wit, immersed in and sharply observing his life and those who have touched it." And poet Dan Gerber called his long-time friend "a wizard of compassion, wisdom—and the seamless fabric between them—in the guise of a comedian. While we are laughing or dazzled, a wise and caring presence is filling and softening our hearts, taking us on flights of the imagination which land in a new place we are surprised to discover is the kingdom of our better selves. Quite simply, his poems nurture our desire to go on living."

An accomplished fiction writer, librettist, singer-songwriter, and actor, Barry Spacks was also an artist who had numerous shows in and around Santa Barbara. He died in Santa Barbara in 2014 at the age of 82.

Spacks Street

Fame: fame: whole generations
going up in pique, uncalled,
unchosen! Silly to waste much strength
earning a place of note (there's not
a grave without
its certified *has-been*)
but once...I wanted a star in my name;
or a state, a river, a unit of measure...
a street, at least...Spacks Street...Spacks Place...
how nice! Imagine the little kids
playing Giant Steps after dinner in summer,
leaping from one of your curbs to the other.
Or someone moves, does well, gains weight
and years and accolades, and says
"God, if they only could see me today,
the old gang
back on Spacks Street!"

What Breathes Us

Regards to the day, the great long day
that can't be hoarded, good or ill.
What breathes us likely means us well.

We rise up from an earthly root
to seek the blossom of the heart.

What breathes us likely means us well.
We are a voice impelled to tell
where the joining of sound and silence is.
We are the tides, and their witnesses.
What breathes us likely means us well.

The Hope of the Air

Michael, trapping a wasp in a cup,
opened the window it battered against
and tossed it free.

        So each of us
unable to find our own release
at times as incomprehensibly
are thrown from the darkness
by who knows what grace
into the hope of the air.

Within Another Life

Those whose days were grudging or confused
may come back trapped within another life
as a boulder, or a pane of glass,
or a door that suffers every time it's slammed.
If I return a boulder, love, some summer day
come sit by me and contemplate these horses and these hills.
And if a windowpane, gaze through to see
the meadow on our walks where the brown geese strut.
And if I am a door, come home through me,
be sure I'll keep you safe.
And if a knotted, twisted rope,
from long self-clenching and complexity,
oh love, unbind, unbraid me then
until I flow again like windswept hair.

An Emblem of Two Foxes (Spacks Street)

Simply to breathe
can make him bleed,
the fox whose leg
is trapped, whose will
awaits the kill.
Why should he flail?
Moving hurts,
so he lies still.

Around him walks
a prouder fox,
his severed leg
a homily
on going free,
as if to say
it hurts, it hurts
either way.

Whitewater Vision

Like everyone else I've served my time
lying under the weight of a mountain,
breathing stones…yet always my blood,
like leveling water, knows where it's wanted.

Once I had a whitewater vision:
beneath the rage of the rapids I sensed
the undersound to the river's sound…
indistinguishable from silence.

Who am I? Not a solving…a seeing.
I view the storm through eyes of calm.
I speak to say
where the silence is.

On days when it seems the food for the journey
is clay, not bread, and the spirit famished,
as dusk transfigures everything
I pause, near silence: listening.

At 35

Father, what would you make of me? I wear your face.
I hear my cough and think the worms have sent you home.
Here at my table in my insubstantial house,
your myth of hope,
The piece of man you left,
I live your death
stroke for stroke.

There are no vows you did not keep I will not break.
I leave no darkness unacknowledged for your sake.
You are the school I teach. The course I take.
I move toward age, and you become my son.
Along the path ahead
you lift aside
the branches.

Buddha Songs

To gaze into an empty room
is not becoming Buddha.
To feed a starving lion, Buddha
gave up one of his precious lives.
As a rabbit, as food,
he leapt in the fire.
We're paired to help,
like hands, like feet.
To gaze into an empty room
is not becoming Buddha.
*

What's loveable about a hum?
Needlessness. It stops, or continues.
Our shadows lie
on a moving stream.
Beautiful…to be beautiful
is all we need to offer each other.
This my cat knows,
and my trees.

The Cow

for Jean Pedrick

The cow's a sort of bourgeois beast:
her peer the steer becomes a feast,
it doesn't faze her in the least;
she'd hardly pause to moo "How triste."

To please the latin sporting crowd
the noble bull, once snorting proud,
is gored by sword, his great head bowed...
and does the cow's contentment cloud?

Of all life's horrors, here's the chief:
her calf's made suede and baby-beef;
the cow displays no signs of grief,
she's stony as a bas-relief.

Her kin can't win? That's Nature's scheme.
At mulling cud the cow's supreme.
While others battle, mourn, blaspheme,
in narcissistic self-esteem

she stands there, giving heavy cream.

2007–2009

PERIE LONGO

Perie Longo

While Barry Spacks's selection as Santa Barbara's first Poet Laureate was roundly approved, there *were* other poets under consideration, chief among them Perie Longo, and her investiture in April of 2007 was met with much celebration by the poetry community. Like Spacks, Longo is a long-time resident of Santa Barbara, who is perhaps best known to two generations of Santa Barbara citizens as a teacher in the Poets in the Schools program and the Santa Barbara Writers Conference, where she has led poetry workshops for almost three decades.

The first two Poets Laureate were good friends, but their work is markedly different. Where Spacks's poems are often brief and aphoristic, Longo's are expansive and filled with "the things of the world"; indeed, Spacks called her "a singer in the Whitmanian mode." And while Spacks was urban and urbane, much more likely sport a pair of blue suede shoes than hiking boots, Longo frequently draws inspiration from close observation of the natural world. A devoted and generous friend, she is also renowned for her sharp wit and that admixture of compassion and acerbity emerge in poems that often respond with a decidedly progressive and pacifist bent to current political events.

Perie Longo has published four books of poetry: *Milking The Earth* (1986), *The Privacy Of Wind* (1997), *With Nothing Behind But Sky: A Journey through Grief* (2006) and *Baggage Claim* (2014). Her work has appeared in *Askew, Atlanta Review, Connecticut Review, International Poetry Review, Nimrod, Paterson Literary Review, Prairie Schooner, Rattle*, and others. Her poems are also included in the anthologies *A Ritual to Read Together: Poems in Conversation with William Stafford, Breathe: 101 Contemporary Odes, Café Solo 3: Central Coast Poets Say What Needs to be Said*, and *Fishing With My Father*.

In addition to teaching for the Santa Barbara Writers Conference, for the past fifteen years she has led the Santa Barbara Poetry Workshop, which she founded.

A psychotherapist in private practice, Longo is a past president of the National Association for Poetry Therapy, which awarded her the Outstanding Achievement Award (1998) and Distinguished Service Award (2004). The Association of Women in Communication, Santa Barbara Chapter, honored her as the Woman of Achievement (2012). Her many travels took her to Kuwait in 2005 where she spoke on Poetry as a Pathway to Peace. She is currently poetry chair of the Nuclear Age Peace Foundation.

Los Angeles Times columnist Charles Champlin said of Longo's second book, *The Privacy of Wind*, "Everything that seems to me the essence of really good poetry is here...with, deep feelings and the gift of conveying those feelings to the reader with heartbreaking power." Glenna Luschei, a fellow poet and the founder of Solo Press, believes, "her poems transport us across the spectrum of emotion: tragic and cathartic to funny and hopeful." And Long Beach poet Gerald Locklin wrote: "Her intelligence, sympathies, music-making and imagery are welded by experienced craft into seamless products of a true poet's art."

Student Poetry Recitation:
Santa Barbara Courthouse Mural Room

Tonight, we complain about the lack of light,
battle with our notes, check if all the contestants
have arrived to recite their memorized poems
in a room larger than life
where justice may be done, lined with murals
of conquistadors on horseback, bent on victory.

How will we see our notes? How will the video film
these bright faces within these solemn walls?
But nothing can stop the students. Soon they are up
reciting Keats and Shakespeare,
Dickinson's "Hope is a thing with feathers,"

all dressed up for poetry's stakes
and you think this was the way of connection
before these murals and that siege, before plagues,
before terrorists and weapons of mass destruction,
and the latest war that turns

East Beach into a sea of white crosses marching
to the wash that drowns our sins,
before all that happens in any life
fevers the pen into action.

So thinking, the students give voice to Momaday
and Millay and while the judges tally the scores,
members of the audience stand to join them

with poems embedded in memory: Chinese and Spanish,
Arabic and Dutch. In this feast of courage,
no matter who's annihilating whom,
hope rears its head in some kind of poetic justice.

The Way of Santa Barbara

> *The wind is the 'breath of the world,'*
> *the means by which the earth and the*
> *human connect with one another.*
>   A Chumash belief

Eyes stinging from the latest backcountry fire,
we lovers of this land, strung between mountain and sea,
lean skyward, scan the horizon, pray the winds breathe back
toward the forest of our fathers, Los Padres, not destroying
what we cherish but saving what matters most—
each other, preserving what we can. In this moment

we are one with all who dwelt here before,
the Chumash and Spanish, Mestizos, Chinese, Italian,
not exempt from Nature's wrath, not exempt from the struggle
to survive in Paradise. This has always been the way
of Santa Barbara, since 1782 when the Presidio rose
in the name of Spain to house and protect new colonists,

and today to understand what happened here. To honor.
In the courtyard, kneeling inside an unearthed well, excavators
scrape clay from a cast iron stove with precision of surgeons,
not to break apart any found object, a piece of pottery
or porcelain, bone or tool. Over their shoulders King Carlos III
stands looking on, smoke plumes rising above.

Perhaps a signal, the site itself rebuilt from rubble and ash
brick by adobe brick, a reminder that to know who we are
we must dig down to the deepest level. The dust on our feet

is the dust of ancestors who ran ahead of the wind.
We stand in beauty, a little short of breath, blood
between us strong—as history teaches—restoring hope.

"What Do Women Want?"

from the diary of Dr. Sigmund Freud

We want to be rain and thunder
      want our voices to summon
         sustenance from our battered earth
we want to be heard in the sheaves of wheat
the rustle of scarves

want to fling a stone of hope in the still pond,
watch ripples pulse across the great divide

want to step from behind war's shadow
      want to be sun, gather and stand
         in gardens we've planted, firmly rooted,
up to our ears in green, rich in food
that bulges from each mound
         and
         heavy
         branch

we hack back vines that choke us all
      open windows in walls, open doors
         through which we freely come and go
and return without dodging snipers
without running away from our lives

may we never again give birth to martyrs
        flown home without limbs or vision
        everywhere women want to be whole together
make stew, simmer all that is true
in the broth of human goodness, invite

every man, woman and child to toss in
        a favored spice, a wish, a way to rebuild
        our fractured world and with tomorrow
in our wombs, we will carry bowls of peace
from hearth to each table, however remote
                this is
                what we
                want

The Age When Anything Is Possible

The fifth grade class doesn't know what a crocus is
that pushes over a mound of snow in spring,
      I explain a tiny cup-like flower that grew in front
of my house in Wisconsin where I lived, their age.

The boy who-only-likes-sports, never poetry,
in a sky blue tank top down to his knees stops wiggling.
Freezes. "Wisconsin!
Did you know my cousin?"

He's ten and serious, lived in Oconomowoc.
A girl says her mother was from Waukesha.
Native words I love wobbling in air, it's time
to write the lesson. Music on, paper passed around
and pictures for ideas,
he appears before me, eyes round as baseballs. Whispers,
      "He was murdered!"
It's not the sun that makes him squint back tears.

Tells me his cousin was twenty-two,
tells me it happened when he was eight,
      the age when life is limitless, anything possible
            but death,
tells me he's scared, they never found who did it.

These days you can't hug children at school, without
    suspicion. I hold him
in my gaze, say I'm sorry, so terrible for him, his family.
Say he could bring his cousin back to the page,
  his pencil like a small bat that sends out words
    where they need to go.

He drifts back to his desk. Writes fast about setting sun
you can't stop, like sadness, morning light, his cousin
  who taught him how to play football,
  that *life won't last forever*. I nod, pass on

tending to others, small flowers bright in their square
  of ground, feet planted
  before they blow away.

Thirst: Kuwait Poetry Workshop

Humans are not our enemies.
  —Thich Nhat Hanh

Out of the silence of writing, she flies
to the front of the lecture hall like a raven,
black swirled around her head, draped
over body, her eyes mirror and shadow, beauty

and anguish at once. In her hand a scrap
of paper like a sail, her words a wind
that propels, released when I spoke
how Rumi wrote to greet every feeling
as guest to the house of the heart.

The veil that covers her mouth vibrates
with each breath, a tent opening
in the desert between us.

Hidden, not heard, she aches with loss,
relatives murdered for war's intolerable gain.
When I ask what can I do,
she tears the veil from her mouth.

Say more. I have such thirst.
Sand becomes water
we drink and drink.

What We Live For...

> *Every time I write a poem I fall in love with it...*
> Anonymous, fourth-grader

...the musk that opens static ducts, press of pine
needles soft on the small of the back, his eyes
full of you, the breath in—his, the breath out—yours,
how the hushed forest awoke when your song
scattered the meadowlarks into the blank, blue sky,
the water's pulse against the banks. With your favorite pen
in hand, the one whose ink flows across the flesh

of the page, you scribble how pear blossoms catch
in the wind like snowflakes, settle on the tips
of winter's brown twigs. You're swimming in words,
one against the other, pull back and they chase
and catch you, together you trace back roads of memory
as the lover's fingers remind you what is true,
no truce until you focus, give your all, release. Child,

the poem you birthed, folded in your pocket, is what
we live for, drives us mad, what one day saves us.

Dedication

Douglas Family Preserve, Santa Barbara

Here you may walk in peace.
Here you may walk in time and history.
Here you may experience an ancient beauty.
Here the community said yes,
this place is ours to preserve,
this precious wind of trails through native plants.
Here you may lose yourself in oak and cypress,
bend to wildflower and lift to the song of ocean breeze
through pine. Here you may watch the sun ease down
over the horizon and at night feel the brush of owl wings.
Through the people of Santa Barbara's generous spirit
and ability to prevail, here you may find yourself.

The Veil

You know how one sock of a pair vanishes
in the laundry while you trim dead branches
in a draught, or make a list of what to do
on Monday? Your hand runs around the inner drum
of the dryer checking to see if it's plastered there
like a dead fish. I read in a book titled *Singlettes*
these socks meander to the "hozone layer."
If so, our departed loved ones are walking around
in the afterlife wearing only a sock—
I found one of his under the couch in search
of a favorite pen—wove it like a flag.
"Come and get it!" That night under full moon
I heard the wind laugh as it grazed a corner
of our home. We talk about the veil between
 life and death thin as a whistle, a whisper,
> a crack in the atmosphere.

Trouble is, everything disappears
once you cross it.

Something Small

Let me write something small
to fit into this large life
or something large
to fit into my small life

or something bold to help me
find strength
like my husband's last breath
or yesterday's red sunset behind
the black peaks

or was it the black peaks
leaning against that vast red wall

Self inside self, are you dying
like the sun or more alive than ever
waiting for the light?

2009–2011

DAVID STARKEY

While he had been actively publishing his poetry since the mid-1980's, David Starkey did not move to Santa Barbara until 2000. However, his work was known to Barry Spacks and David Oliveira (see Coda), and they welcomed him into the local scene. Starkey also benefited from the fact that several years after moving to Santa Barbara, he began hosting an arts interview program, *The Creative Community*, which aired in heavy rotation on local TV. Whatever his relative merits as a poet might have been, his face was familiar to the people of Santa Barbara.

Poet Lawrence Raab wrote that "David Starkey's inventive poems are funny and serious in equal measure, and happily unafraid to adjust what seem to be the world's truths to go after something a little stranger, and a little more true." This constant bouncing back and forth between comedy and tragedy, low culture and high, is characteristic of much of Starkey's work. A poet of place, he has written extensively about wherever he has lived: from his hometown of Sacramento to Los Angeles, Baton Rouge, rural South Carolina, suburban Chicago, northern Finland and Rome. Therefore, it was no surprise that one of his major projects as Poet Laureate was a series of poems about Santa Barbara—the subject of each poem being suggested by a Santa Barbara citizen—which were subsequently filmed and aired on television and online as "Santa Barbara Poems."

David Starkey directs the Creative Writing Program at Santa Barbara City College, where he is Professor of English. He has published seven full-length collections of poetry, most recently *It Must Be Like the World* (Pecan Grove, 2011), *Circus Maximus* (Biblioasis, 2013) and *Like a Soprano* (Serving House, 2014), an episode-by-episode revisioning of *The Sopranos* TV series. In addition, over the past twenty-eight years he has published more than 400 poems in literary journals such as *Alaska Quarterly Review, American Scholar, Antioch Review, Barrow Street,*

Georgia Review, Massachusetts Review, Notre Dame Review, Poetry East, Southern Review, Southern Humanities Review, and *Southern Poetry Review. Creative Writing: Four Genres in Brief* (Bedford/St. Martin's) will soon be in its third edition and is currently one of the best-selling creative writing textbooks in North America.

Reviewing Starkey's work in *The Georgia Review*, Paul Zimmer praised his "wonderful language" and "amazing lines," concluding, "Starkey is an entertaining and resourceful poet." David Kirby wrote that "the great philosophers weave in and out of these poems, hand in hand with the great criminals, and David Starkey is a step behind them, missing nothing." And Eloise Klein Healy found Starkey's poems to be "awash with reports from the senses and in full-throated song about it all. Wise, witty, and wide-ranging, this is poetry that will reward the reader with the kind of delight one feels in the face of masterwork."

The Difference Between Poets and Politicians

I, who have voted in every election
since turning eighteen, honor the work
of public servants, your devotion
to the larger cause, your willingness
to sit through meetings that might send me
screaming from the room. Poets,
you understand, are different. We see
a tree and rather than *environment*
or *public park*, think *willow*
or *coral* or *flowering pear*.
To us, fire evokes metaphors
as soon as terror, the mountains
at dusk are *crepuscular*,
the ocean is a *vasty deep*.
For you, problems are opportunities
for solutions; for us, they are occasions
for elegies and light verse. Nothing
moves poets like ambiguity:
upright Portia's sudden cruelty,
the pathos we feel for Shylock,
though he insisted on his pound of flesh.
We swim in shades of gray and green
and aquamarine. Therefore, I receive
these laurels humbly, realizing the most
that I can likely do on your behalf is mark
a moment on the calendar, then order
the Number Six lunch special at Pepé's,
breathe in the scent of blooming jasmine,
and chant the euphonious names—
Anacapa, de la Vina, Camino
Manadero—of our lovely city's streets...

Lawnmower

So lazy that long ago summer, I had it coming. Dad had been after
>me all day to cut the grass and clean the living room. *Just two
>goddamn things*, he swore before slamming shut my door, *that's
>all I ask*. But I was busy back then with my Zeppelin records and
>phone calls to my girlfriend, Pet. I let it slide.

I was so wasted last night, Pet was moaning during our third
>conversation of the morning, when a bomb detonated
>downstairs. *What's that?!* Pet yipped, but I'd already dropped
>the receiver, started toward the noise, a raspy roar that hadn't
>stopped.

From the landing I saw Mom and my sister standing on the sofa,
>holding hands and screaming as Dad wheeled the lawnmower
>across our thick gold shag. It took me several moments to absorb.
>He'd set the wheels as low as they could go, so the carpet itself,
>not just my rock star magazines, *Creem* and *Rolling Stone*, my
>unfinished homework, my paper plates of half-eaten snacks, the
>soda cans, the junk mail I was saving to sort through someday, all
>of it came shooting from the blower into the air like grass.

Carl! Mom yelled, *Carl, Carl, stop!* but he was starting on a footstool
>when my sister, who later became a nurse, leapt and pulled the
>sparkplug wire. The roaring guttered out. Nothing—but the air
>conditioner's hum, two kids playing outside.

I came down, silent, and began picking up the mess. Mom put her arms around her husband. My sister went upstairs. I was nearly finished when I glanced over and saw him crying, the one thing he'd told me a boy could never do. Mom, mascara running, hissed, angrier than I'd ever heard her: *Not a word from you, mister. Not a word until you understand.*

Spring Flowers

I miss the comfort in being sad.
—Kurt Cobain, "Frances Farmer Will Have Her Revenge on Seattle"

April 1994 and the children
of Seattle are bereaved.
The one man who seemed
really to understand them
has blown his brains out
with a shotgun. In flannel
shirts they gather to sing
his dirges, throw syringes
on makeshift altars of candles
and cards, Narcissus and daffodils.

Meanwhile, back in Rwanda,
where bullets are a luxury,
young men use clubs to cave in
skulls, machetes to hack off
arms and legs and heads. One
by one, those hiding in churches
are plucked from sanctuary,
marched to the cemeteries
and killed. Gladiolas flame
along the roadside in the rain.

In South Carolina, I brood
in my two-bedroom home

with my three children and my bi-
polar wife, mourning my own
miserable life through poetry.
Already it's ninety degrees
in the afternoon, dogwood
blooming, yellow jasmine
running up the phone poles,
tulips bursting as if from pain.

A Few Things You Should Know about the Finns

Their preferred seasons are summer—the moon
fat, low and brief in the sky—and autumn,
just before winter arrives, when the leaves
haven't yet fallen and cattle still roam free.
Winter, the great constant, is not a favorite,
it is a fact. If a tree is in their way,
they hack it down. They believe the sea is always
slate gray and that there is a stoicism,
a kind of morality in stone.
Alone in each other's company, they often
find themselves silent, although there is much
that they would say, if the words didn't fall
just out of reach and evaporate, like snowflakes
shaken from a coat onto a cast-iron stove.

What the Sea Can Hold

for Mary Dan Eades, Perie Longo and Barbara Bell

A chorus of ethereal voices? Of course.
Mere orchestras—with their bassoons
and trombones, their tubas and triangles—
are nothing to its enormity. The sea
can hold any number of symphonies.

It contains whales and washing machines,
tires and albacore tuna, plankton
and the odd plank afloat somewhere
in the Pacific, five hundred miles
from the nearest atoll's shore. It cradles

the moon in its waves and embraces
each whim of the fickle wind, that demon
lover every sailor woos and fears. Ships
the size of small cities sink anonymously
into its trenches: Mariana and Tonga,

Yap and Diamantina: they vanish
into the abyss of the Cayman Trough
and into the Calypso Deep, leaving only
blackness behind. And yet the sea holds
words and chanteys and the ashes

of those we love and who loved her.
It may grow bleak and barren,
but for all its surprises, it never fails
to come about. Listen to its cadences:
every retreating tide promises a return.

In Praise of the Public Library

for Jinny Webber

Where would we go if not here,
this place of astonishment
and weightlessness, where
our floodlit eyes—readjusting
to the interior—focus
on the slow, Zen-like attention
of the browsers, clattering
of fingers on keyboards,
the muddled lives of individuals
intersecting with the clutter
of history, which diligent hands
have untangled and classified:
art married with recreation,
philosophy sharing space
with psychology, economics
nudging up against the law.
Fiction stands alone, of course—
there is so much of it: pooling
in obscure corners, wispy
as the reasoning that runs
through so many of our favorite
books, slumbering among the sleepers
who have wobbled in from the unkind
streets. If you, too, shut your eyes,
you will hear the rustle of newspapers,

the rasping wheels of the reshelving
carts, the questions answered
and the murmur of those
unresolved. Above it all,
the musical chattering of children
rising like a soprano's descant—
their voices not yet trained to silence.

Bibliothèque du Soleil

—Destroyed, January 12, 2010

A reader will find her book, though it is buried
Certain fathoms beneath the uncertain surface

Of the earth, though its pages are torn like feathers
From a fowl and drenched with dust. The shelves

May remain empty for a time, leaving the reader
Bereft of her books, but a book finds its way

Home to its reader, persistently, quietly, like a song
After singing, like sun beyond clouds.

The unquenchable thirst of a mind
Blazing with the incandescent need to find

Again her book, will unearth first the one,
Then the others, until the words roil like spring

Water rising, like spirits set free at the crossroads
To transform the knell summoning sorrow

Into the chimes of church bells and the coming
Of help and to pages and pages of tomorrow.

—For Nadège Clitandre

Nuns in Rome

       So wonderful to see them here
              in their gray wimples and habits
and sensible shoes, giggling
         like the schoolgirls whose hands
     they're obliged to slap, delighted
             when some tourist deigns
    to take their photograph
in front of Saint Peter's
        or the Pantheon. Most

    seem to be visitors, like me,
              stockpiling memories
of the Eternal City against
       their inevitable return
    to Nairobi or Bratislava
             or Asunción. Heavy work
    awaits them—dictators
and poverty and ravenous priests
       who cannot wolf down

    the local lads fast enough—
            but for the moment shafts
of sunlight slice occasionally
       into the narrow streets, or shine
    on the piazzas where boys
            kick soccer balls at the walls
    of the ancient churches—Santa Barbara
dei Librari, Chiesa Nuova, la Basilica
       di Santa Maria del Popolo.

Fire-following Flowers

—For Sharon and Paul

      This past summer, when I almost lost my house
            to fire, I vowed to appreciate
        the things left to me. Yet this winter, when
you lost yours, it seemed presumptuous
      to assume might-have-been compared with what is.

        Still, as spring approaches, we should recall
that the capricious earth witnesses,
      always, renewal. The arroyo

     lupine and the golden efflorescence
            that is Spanish broom, the slender Mariposa
      lily and the starfish-shaped and deadly
star lily, the waxy leafed soap plant
     and the twirly vines of the wild cucumber,

        the wooly yarrow and the yucca plant—
also known as Our Lord's candle and Spanish
      bayonet—deerweed and beardtongue and the many-

     blossomed snapdragon will explode in a chaos
           of orange, yellow, lavender, white and blue
        across the steep slopes of our hills, which even now
are turning green. Perhaps, when you're hiking
      above the place your home once stood,

        you'll look down through the scrub oak and chinquapin
and glimpse a memory—a backyard barbecue,
    the driveway where your daughter learned to balance

    on her bike. Maybe you'll pick a fire poppy
          and pluck its pumpkin-colored petals
      while you wait for the moment to pass.
Maybe the air will thrum with bees
    and the towhee's *here-here-here-please*.

      Possibly you will look at one another
and say, without speaking, that the most
    difficult times are sometimes lovely, too.

2011–2013

Paul J. Willis

Paul J. Willis

Paul J. Willis, Santa Barbara's fourth Poet Laureate, is both a scholar and an outdoorsman. He grew up in Oregon, attended Wheaton College in Illinois, worked as a mountain guide in the Cascades and Sierra Nevada, and earned his graduate degrees at Washington State University, where he wrote a dissertation on *The Forest in Shakespeare: Setting as Character*.

That combination of erudition and clear-eyed reportage on the phenomena of the natural world is seasoned by Willis's quiet but deep beliefs as a Christian. To say that his work is carefully crafted—it certainly is—would be to miss the passion for both the physical and spiritual world that is at the heart of his best poetry. Indeed, one suspects Willis, with his keen eye and ear, could write brilliantly about anything—in heaven, or here on our "beautiful, suffering world."

Paul Willis is a professor of English at Westmont College in Santa Barbara, where he has taught creative writing and British Renaissance literature since 1988. With David Starkey, he edited the anthology *In a Fine Frenzy: Poets Respond to Shakespeare* (University of Iowa Press, 2005). His work in creative nonfiction is *Bright Shoots of Everlastingness: Essays on Faith and the American Wild* (WordFarm, 2005), and his three full collections of poems are *Visiting Home* (Pecan Grove Press, 2008), *Rosing from the Dead* (WordFarm, 2009), and *Say This Prayer into the Past* (Cascade Books, 2013). He is also the author of an eco-fantasy quartet, *The Alpine Tales* (WordFarm, 2010), portions of which were previously published as separate novels by Avon Books.

Willis's poems and essays have appeared in well over a hundred journals, including *Poetry*, *Image*, and *Wilderness*, and have also been anthologized in *The Best American Poetry 1996* (Scribner's), *The Best Spiritual Writing 1999* (HarperSanFrancisco), *The Best American Spiritual Writing 2004* (Houghton Mifflin), and *The Best Christian Writing 2006* (Jossey-Bass). More recently his poems have been featured on *Verse Daily* and *The Writer's Almanac*.

His poetry chapbook *The Deep and Secret Color of Ice* was selected for the Small Poetry Press Prize in 2002 by Jane Hirshfield, who said of his work, "Paul Willis's poems give off a multifaceted, sharp-edged beauty, akin to the light that sometimes glints from the edges of leaves after rain. They look to the places where unexpected treasures lie quietly hidden—a childhood illness, a set of old wooden bleachers, a Sierra Juniper's berries—and bring that treasure richly forward, into a mature, and maturing wisdom."

Just after Groundhog Day

Just after Groundhog Day, summer begins
in Santa Barbara. Keen smells of blossoms
layer the air, the yellow bloom of mustard
weed and sourgrass and acacia fulfilling
their own prophecy on every side.

Frogs erupt in the barranca,
and out by the mailbox where we linger
to talk in the evening, mosquitoes
gather to be with us, flitting
against the silhouette of the islands
at the foot of the street.

All is latent, luscious, languorous,
the tall grass under the oaks
already thick and green and shining.

Mornings in May could be like this in Oregon
when I got up to deliver papers on my bike.
The houses slept amidst a waking of everything
that was young again—the river, the sky,
the bigleaf maples—while I flung the news
like birdsong, end over end to every doorstep.

A Story of Hands

Our hands, say the Chumash,
were supposed to be coyote paws.

Coyote had won the argument
of who would provide that part of us.

At the last second, lizard,
who had been very quiet,

reached out to touch the white
stone of our creation in the sky

and left his print. That's why
our hands are lizard hands.

That's why lizard keeps diving
down into cracks in the rock.

Coyote is still wanting
to get his paws on him.

Midsummer

This evening we are awash in light.
   It buoys the mountains as if they have finally
     found their proper medium, their true home,

as if only now the peaks and ridges
   and chaparral have come to the surface
     and are free to look around, to take in air,
       to catch us up in their respiration.

If only we could bathe ourselves
   in light like this the whole year through.
     Could we survive, amidst so much joy?

This evening is the highest tide,
   the crest of possibility.
     All ships come in:
       hulls sleek, sails shining.

Extra Innings

From a shaky scaffold rising out of the poison oak,
a pair of men are tearing off
the back of our redwood baseball stands.

Who would have guessed it?
Between the boards, row on row of honeycombs,
packed in like a visiting team in brown and saffron uniforms.

All these years a sweetness
building at our backs, a hidden infield
of play, the score kept in numberless columns

by so many runs home. Here was a game
never called on account of darkness,
only halted by too much light.

Intercession

When I wake in the night and think
of what I might have said in class that day,
I wonder why my life consists

of inarticulate occasions.
No timely word, only belated ones.
Every hour a first draft, and then another.

It makes me want to announce, "Listen!
Listen to what I do not say. Listen
to what it is you cannot say yourselves."

There are sighs and groans,
    just sighs and groans.
Interpret them, dear ones, as you may.

On City Council

There's a way of getting here.
You walk door-to-door, shake hands,
say things into a microphone.

The night comes when you sit
in a restaurant with your friends
and watch the numbers on the screen.

Then you go home and think about
being in this room again on a Tuesday—
or being here for the first time.

That's when it hits you:
you worked for this, and now you have it—
a bit of trust from some of your neighbors,

the chance to decide a thing or two.
And you realize how lucky you are,
how good it is to clear a space

and roll up your collective sleeves,
here, now, on this curved dais
above the creaking pews of the public.

What We Have

There are still fall colors here, even in Santa Barbara:
the bright crimson of toyon berries, clustered
against the paling sky, the chartreuse mottling
of sycamore leaves and yellowing rust of bay,

of laurel. Along each path, bleached memories
of poison oak, a hardening of its arteries
while tender grass appears behind
November rains. And in the high folds of the ridge,

well above the waterfalls and already hidden
from the sea, the inland bloom of cottonwoods,
holding up their blazing hands
and giving all they owe to the wind.

Refugio

The palm-lined beach is hollow in its sweep,
the point break spins the rollers long and slow;
one surfer pulls a headstand on his board,
approaching sand as sky, and sky as sand.

In December 1812 a tidal wave
snapped a Boston ship, *The Mercury*, from anchor
and sent it surging inland up the creek
a full half mile, rushing through the tops
of sycamore, through groves of flooded oak.

Between the hills the water lost its force
and sucked itself backrushing to the sea,
the schooner with it, sliding swift, intact,
the sailors at the rails, amazed with fear,
but certain, if they made it past the shore,
that nothing else in their reverted lives
could ever really take them by surprise.

On the 225th Year of Mission Santa Barbara

(1786-2011)

After our house burned down in the Tea Fire,
we rented a place on Laguna Street a few blocks
below the Mission. In the mornings I'd walk
the dog to the rose garden and through the high grass
of the meadow underneath the bell towers,
desperately in need of their blessing.

I took comfort in knowing they had been there
for a long time, shadowing others in their search
for certainty, for something in their lives that would stay.
Oh, I know those towers crumbled in an earthquake in 1925,
and whatever had preceded them was reduced
to rubble in 1812. And I also know that the Chumash
were not altogether grateful to be herded into these precincts
and forced to build that fern-covered dam on the creek.

And the long abuse of those boys at the school—
I know about that too. But driving home from work
that winter, I often chose the longer route
that brought me down the canyon to that graceful turn
around those towers rising above the rusty leaves
of sycamore in the last of the sun, my gaze
falling across the lawn to the tile rooftops of our city,
the ocean beyond, the islands glinting like a promise.

And I would think of those many friars, most of them
so patient and humble, so full of faith, so dedicated

Paul J. Willis

to those who came to place their burdens on the warm stone
of these steps that lead out from that sanctuary
to the rest of this beautiful, suffering world.

2013–2015

Chryss Yost

Chryss Yost

Chryss Yost served as Santa Barbara's fifth poet laureate. A writer of carefully wrought, formally intricate poems, Yost had for many years been a significant presence on the local scene, hosting and organizing events, including the Santa Barbara Poetry Series. Perhaps most importantly for the community, she was instrumental in shaping Santa Barbara's April Poetry Month by creating an annual calendar that lists all the independently-organized events in one place. Her natural modesty may have precluded her from making a more forceful argument for the laureateship, but by 2013, Yost's fellow poets felt strongly that it was her turn to be crowned with the laurel wreath.

Like Barry Spacks, Yost tends to write a shorter, highly musical poem. However, whereas Spacks's poems tend to finish on a note of Buddhist wisdom, Yost's poetry more often tends toward the inconclusive and ambiguous. There is a delicacy to her poems, yet the lines themselves are strong, polished, sinewy.

During her laureateship, Yost continued her work on behalf of the community, founding the Shoreline Voices Project at Gunpowder Press. Books published by the Shoreline Voices Project are collaborations with local institutions and include Santa Barbara-area poets writing on a common theme. Another of her passions is creating opportunities for emerging poets, students, and English-language learners to participate alongside more established poets. An example of a favorite collaboration was a poster project she helped to curate. Organized by the Contemporary Arts Forum, the posters, featuring poems in English and Spanish by local elementary school students, were displayed in MTD buses for several years.

Born in San Diego, Yost is a lifelong Californian who has lived in Santa Barbara since 1990. She attended Santa Barbara City College as a re-entry student before transferring to UCSB, where she majored in English and minored in professional writing. While at UCSB, she received awards for her business writing, fiction, and poetry. Her poems have been set to music and she is a frequent collaborator with artists and galleries: she has written poems on request for the Santa Barbara Museum of Art, the County Arts Commission, the Museum of Natural History, and Sullivan Goss Gallery. Her poem "Furious Bread" was selected for the 2014 Patricia Dobler Poetry Award by Patricia Smith.

Since publishing her first poems in a national journal in 1997, Yost has published two fine-press chapbooks and has co-edited major poetry anthologies, including *California Poetry: From the Gold Rush to the Present* (co-edited with California Poet Laureate Dana Gioia and Jack Hicks). While serving as Poet Laureate, her first full-length book, *Mouth & Fruit*, was published by Gunpowder Press. She has since become a co-editor at the press, which is named to honor Barbara of Nicomedia, patron saint of gunpowder.

California poet laureate Al Young wrote: "*Mouth & Fruit*—what a hearty debut! If ever there lived a hands-on poet, her name is Chryss Yost. Wired with feeling and touch, reverie and thought, anger and hunger, these sleek poems dart, dive, sizzle, and sometimes sting." And Colorado poet laureate Dave Mason said, "Chryss Yost's poems are like the coastal light of California, so brightly made you almost miss the grief between the lines. This is poetry of warm intelligence, sensuality and grace."

Eduardo Recites Keats' "Ode on a Grecian Urn"

2013 Santa Barbara County Poetry Out Loud competition

I don't know how Eduardo chose the ode.
    50 lines—so much to memorize,
to stand up and recite before a crowd.
    It is an old poem for an ancient vase,
English Romantic poetry at its height,
    all nymphs and pipers and rhapsodies.
Eduardo adjusts the mic. His tie looks tight.

Thou still unravish'd bride of quietness!
    Thou foster-child of silence and slow time

He begins. The words blossom with his voice.
    They have been growing in him all winter,
between school, stadium, work, and home
    between fields and fossil-striped stone,
beyond them, vineyards, oaks and oceans.
    Collapsing, connecting Greece to London,
Santa Barbara, two hundred years later.
    The imagined kiss, the unheard song.

"Beauty is truth, truth beauty," – that is all
    Ye know on earth, and all ye need to know.

Before we rise in applause for Eduardo,
there is a moment all seems possible –
    the old poem spoken in a new voice
while the city of Santa Barbara listens,
    beautiful as we will ever be.

The Flow

When the water comes, it brings the mountain
and sings the story of the shifting ridge,
summons green to bloom along its edge.
Shapes the hills with patient excavation.

Water comes and carries what we were:
wind-torn leaves, the old path washed away,
the swallowed reflections of hunter and prey.
Brings ash and remains of the bear flag bear.

When water comes, thirst rises for reunion
with the river. All are sullied by the journey.
What blessing to reclaim our purity,
leave the salty stories for the ocean.

We are renewed, to wonder which came first:
that flow of water or this endless thirst?

California Roots

What glimmers here
        is the sun on the channel
the creek dappled
        in the sycamores' shade
even the wash water,
        murky with the dust
of roads that have yet
        to been named.

This is a place for praise,
        and the work of praising.

The native sycamore
        spreads shallow roots,
finding its miracles
        close to the people,

their new voices
        and scrub jays
given equal attention,

a patchwork of witnesses
        telling their stories.
As leaves whisper
        in the quiet heat,

there is no higher calling
        than to listen.

Furious Bread

The yeast wakes up, faster than sourgrass after the rain.
I warm the old bowl on the pilot light, as my grandmother did,

scrape level the measure of flour using a knife's flat back.
There is no end to stubborn in this world. Even flour

fights like it would rather be grain again, recoils after every stretch,
the dough thick and heavy as a lump of potters' clay.

I push hard, throwing my weight behind each stroke,
arms stiff, lifting on my toes. Flatten, fold, turn, flatten, fold.

The newspaper on the table shows a senator. Resolved,
he says. One man, one woman. His God will not be swayed.

I pound the kneading board, knead until my wrists ache,
my skin crusted with salt, slowly will *yield*, will *suppleness*.

I round the dough to rest in the deep glazed bowl,
wait for rising, baking, food for those who sit at my table.

Naked Ladies at the End of Summer

Like bright thread on a tatted skirt,
they edge the drive: bold, slender,
flirting toward the door, as if to enter,
the queens of July, petaled heads,
yes too thin, too unprepared to leave.
September finds them in retreat, hurt,
Fragile, fading, tired of parading.

Portrait of a Saint with Schwinn and BBQ Sauce

After Niccolo di Buonaccorso's "Saint Lawrence"

I can tell you there was no one more
in love with Jesus than I was one June
when I was I guess about eleven, twelve.

I was pretty much like this guy here.
Everything just me and then the goldness
that was really God and all his love.

I might be riding my bike home and think,
My whole life is a bike ride home to heaven.
Most of what I knew about the Lord

was from Christmas carols and AA
meetings where I sat in back with Mom.
And now this hippy farm church

where a they did the whole pastor-
with-guitar-and-singer-wife scene.
There were a lot of dogs to pet there.

All it took was to say yes to God
and what did I have to lose? Nothing
except my sloth, maybe some coveting.

I tell you, it was bliss to know that He
had a plan and even I was part of it.
Even my peeling scabbed-up sunburn.

I felt it, riding home. My Destiny.
The track clear as a line to follow.
To bike down your street at sunset

and smell the dinner smells and know that
that chicken BBQ is at your own house,
and God has it, all of it, under control

if you just let him into your heart.
Saint Lawrence, I woulda been there
with you and the chicken on the grill,

while the empty-bellied neighbors
crushed their empty Buds and cussed.
wherever He'd wanted me to go,

I'd go singing because he asked.
Those summer loves, they burn,
and He never asked me to.

Wicked

You are the swarm gathering force, collecting
and constructing. I feel the walls rise, warming, fragrant.
The wind stills, what need have we for windows?
This desire, the need of blossoms to be kissed,
for pollen mulled in the mouth like a poem
to be shaped into lotus pods, to be filled with seed,
to open in heat. Lucky wick, surrounded by softening
wax, sweet with the breath of bees.

Lai with Sounds of Skin

Shall we dress in skin,
our living linen?
Bone weft,
pull of masculine
into feminine,
the heft,
the warp, weave and spin
of carded days in

tightly-twisted thin
yarns that we begin—
like wool
like *will*, like *has been*,
spoken to silken—
to spool:
thick bolts of linen,
skein to skin to skin.

Last Night

When the sun sets, and he isn't home, she walks
Not to be waiting, but she leaves a note:
Back soon, her only message, only wish.

After all, she didn't think he'd stay;
No plans, so no surprises when it ends.
The dishes wait unwashed. Bitter stains

Stretch like shadows on the tablecloth.
Once you believe in finding gods in mortal men
You understand their restlessness as faith;

The way she feels his truth against her skin,
The rough edge of a matchbook, while she grieves
To see her saviors lost, and lost again.

God save the church that she takes refuge in,
The sanctuary given fools and thieves,
This silent girl who loves a man who leaves.

2015–2017

SOJOURNER KINCAID ROLLE

The first five Santa Barbara Poets Laureate all emerged from a poetry group begun by Barry Spacks (and which continues to meet monthly after his death), and while the quality of the work being produced by this group, and their commitment to the Santa Barbara community, was never in question, the selection of Sojourner Kincaid Rolle as the city's sixth Poet Laureate undoubtedly ushered in a new era.

Like most of the Santa Barbara Poets Laureate, Rolle has deep roots in the community. In 1993, she was named county-wide "Woman of the Year" by the Santa Barbara County Commission on the Status of Women, and in 1999 she was named "Woman of the Year in Arts" by the Tres Condados Girl Scout Council. In addition to being a poet and playwright, Rolle is an environmental educator and a peace activist, and those twin concerns are evident in much of her work. She also hosts the Poetry Zone readings and has served as both a coach and county-level judge for Poetry Out Loud, a national poetry recitation program for high school students. Consequently, the oral performance of her poetry is central to her aesthetic, and she is known throughout the poetry community as a fiery public speaker. As Poet Laureate, she is passionate about "elevating poetry [and poets] in the eyes of the community."

Rolle's book of poems for young people, *The Mellow Yellow Global Umbrella*, was re-published in 2015 by Lucky Penny Press as its first bilingual poetry book in English and Spanish. Her other books include *Common Ancestry* (Millie Grazie Press, 1999) and *Black Street*, (Center for Black Studies Research, 2009). Her poems have appeared in the journals *California Quarterly*, *Coffee Press*, *Squaw Review* and others, and in the anthologies *The Geography of Home, Rivertalk 2000, Poetry Zone I, II & III, The Poetry of Peace, A Crow Black as the Sun* and *Corners of the Mouth: Celebrating 30 Years of the SLO Poetry Festival*.

As part of her poetry activism, Rolle has engaged young poets through her "Song of Place Poetry Project" and her work with City At Peace, Speak for the Creeks, the Annual Young Writers Poetry Contest and the MLK Poetry and Essay Contest. She is a two-time recipient of the California Arts Council's Artist-in-Community Residency Award and for eight years led poetry workshops in schools throughout the South County as a part of the Santa Barbara Public Library's "English Language Learner's Initiative." Moreover, since 2002 she has organized an annual tribute to Langston Hughes.

Gloria Willingham-Toure, educator and founder of the Village Projects, says of Sojourner Kincaid Rolle: "She writes with a graceful rhythm that transforms the simplest words into a work of art. She is more than a poet, she is poetry. When she gives her words to you it brings your mind, body, and soul to a place that only those so gifted can take you. She speaks on the topic of creative expression in a way that motivates all in her presence to reach deeper into their own lives and to grow from that experience."

A Song of Santa Barbara

We honor the first people of this place:
Chumash, Barbareños.
We honor the elders,
the keepers of this ancient culture.
O' the beautiful city by the sea,
city by the side of the Royal Road.

Stately palms sway in harmony with the wind
and the soaring hawks.

Dancers, yellow hibiscus blossoms
in their hair, twirl and clap.
Magenta bougainvilleas snake along the pathways,
crawl across scape of land,
climb the stucco walls.

In the name of Saint Barbara,
patron of mariners and surfers,
we pay homage to the dolphin
relating the legend of the Rainbow Bridge.

We honor those whose forebears
built a life here.
We know their names.
They are as familiar
as the names off our streets,
our paseos, our placitas:
De la Guerra,
Gutierrez,

Carrillo,
Cota,
Ortega…

We take shelter beneath
the Moreton bay fig,
a canopy of hope.
We hang our holiday lights
on the Norfolk Island pine.

We are known for graceful palm,
the lavender jacaranda,
the California scrub oak.

Caretakers
to the watershed,
we lift our eyes
to hills.
Our creeks—Mission,
Sycamore, Arroyo Burro—
some dry beds,
carry the precious liquid
more valued than gold.

We are keepers of bees.
Hummingbirds flitter
among birds of paradise.

Monarchs graze in our front yards,
traveling the yellow-blossomed coast
clustering in the warm embrace
of our eucalyptus groves.

We share our plenty with the seagulls
and the crows.
We hold sanctuary for the California condor,
the bald eagle, the brown pelican
the snowy plover, the green turtle,
the island fox.

We wake each day
to the sounds of a mixed flock.
Mockingbirds serenade us
through long afternoon into night.

Singing a song of Santa Barbara.

April 7, 2015

A Space Where a Poem Ought to Be

I've known of missing poems before
poems stronger than the suppressing hand
poems more powerful than the invisibility

poems that speak from the realm of the soul
from the place that needs no facade
the place impalpable where the poem touches

a father's unrenderable gaze

absent from the family photograph
frozen in clenched smile abstraction
hovering somewhere near the unfathomable

a hole where a heart once lay

cached between bone and muscle
a conduit for that which makes life livable
its beat but an echo its rhythm but a spasm of memory

hurt where a friendship once was

its demise never anticipated
its loss never contemplated
it measure infinite

space where a leg ought be

the missing limb but bits of flesh femur blood
soft shrapnel on a once abandoned war ground
the mined soil holding secret its maiming terror

nothing where something ought be

it is said that to which the missing was adjoined
the left behind
mourns its disattached
one sees the shining knee—
the favored other

there is emptiness longing
grief is spoken
and desire

Circle of Painted Stones

at La Casa de Maria

Standing in this circle,
we clasp hands.
A momentary silence,
then in hushed reverence,
we honor each stone;
we utter each name;
we hallow each memory.
We salute our common grief.

Gentle clover—beauty's emissary—
encircles each remembrance.

Here among the memory stones,

we consider the years
they might have lived;

consider the hands
that might have worked
toward healing;

consider the feet
that might have strode
out of the dark tunnels
into the light.

Here familiars congregate in
disparate spaces.

On my writing hand,
as if to guide it, a fly lands.

A crow babbles in unison
with the sweet whistle of
a wren. A duet of opposites.

Here we speak a common tongue;
the language of sorrow and loss
and, too, hope.

Hosanna

For the Artists of Santa Barbara

In the quietest of spaces,
On a twig in the hedge;
near a cone at the top
of a Torrey Pine tree;
one chirp begins the sound of day—
the downbeat for a symphony.

On a hillside,
high above the morning wave,
Pacific water rushing in and easing out;
a first brush-stroke begins the great unfolding—
the plein air narrative of this moment.

Somewhere on the land beneath the rocks
where massive middens of abalone and debris
evidence our ancient places on coastal shores,
a dancer lifts one bare foot mocking the slow
deliberate step of a blue heron;
raising a bare leg in the manner of a Sandhill Crane,
lifting a jointed limb like the graceful Snowy Egret.
as if we humans could take flight.

We poets place words in the mouths of crows;
create a language of our own imaginings.
We imagine song as if sparrows were singing.

Sojourner Kincaid Rolle

We imagine dance as if shore birds could touch the sky.
We view the painter's renderings as evidence
of our meanderings—our longings made visible.

Sending up our praises, our hallelujahs, our hosannas.
We embrace the musicians, the dancers, the painters, the poets, the
sculptors, the weavers of thread....
We who create hold common cause.
We honor all that is beautiful.

Inseparable

Not unlike single fingers
Tethered to a common hand,
We are mingled—
Stirred from one vastness.

One air permeates our being.

As a boulder rolls,
As the earth settles,

So too we move and slow.
We sleep and wake;
Dream night and day.

Each moment as soon as spent
Becomes a part of the great our past.

Each breath infinitesimally mingled;
Each drop of dew a composite.

We reach for that one glorious expression
Achieved by our composed action
That our living not be for naught;
That our striving not be in vain.

There are great overcomings:
Going against the tide,
Changing the flow of the river,
Struggling Sisyphean toward triumph.

Some have felt the whole
Power of a nation well up within.
Each of us is called
To our own greater expanse

Let this shining star
Be a sign unto us—
All is not lost,
We bask in reflected glory

And continue.

A Charge To Keep In Mind

There is a charge to keep.
It covers the tree keepers
and those who seek to cut them down.
It covers the pedi-drivers
and those who ride in limousines.
It covers the harbors and the hillsides
the landmarks and the NIMBY's.
In all its disparate ways,
It covers the voter and the non-voter;
equal status in the public square.

Your charge is to your neighbor
your neighbor's water
your neighbor's land use and limits
your neighbor's joyful noise
your neighbor's refuse and effuse
your neighbor's children in the park
your neighbor's safety on the street.

You have a charge to make a way
for walkers, bikers, runners, climbers.
You have a charge to make a place
for swimmers, skaters, dancers, painters.

You have a charge to listen
Be we praisers or critics—

Sojourner Kincaid Rolle

Be we transient or landed
You have a charge to hear us all,
to keep our counsel at heart.

We, the people, are a multitude
many cultures, many creeds, many life ways—
endowed or impoverished, we all marvel at the rainbow.

Today we can begin
    to see a new vision
    to hear with new understanding
    to act in concert toward our common good.
You have a charge to keep.
We have a bond to hold.

An Ode to the King Palm at Anacapa Street

King Palm,
You honor this place
by your being.
Once *Seaforthia Elegans*
now *Archontophoenix*,
chieftain palm.

King Palm,
your like and near kin
line street after street:
Anacapa, Chapala,
Santa Barbara;
cluster along the boulevard
at the ocean.
grace the skyline on the Mesa,
inspire dream vistas on the Riviera.

King Palm,
you stand
singular but not alone,
in a gesture of gratitude;
your proud posture
a thank you to the ones
who envisioned and the ones
who carry the vision.
The ones who make our
city a tree beautiful city.

Where The Hum Begins

I am in a place
where water rolls across the stones
rippling in ranges
too high for human tones to mimic

It is a place
where mountains loom over land
so low it is almost level with the sea

In the distance
I can hear water falling fast
from a high plateau
brushing the slope of the solid earth
at sharp angles, diving
into the flow
where it falls, a continuous splash issues

It is at this place I dwell
between calm and turmoil,
between yang and yin
between memory and amnesia

between today and tomorrow
between sate and want

In the magic hour
when the tide changes
In the right moment

where each second becomes the next
in the pull of the moon
while the water ebbs and flows

In this place, I stand
on land rocky like a river
land where boulders abide
deep within the soil

It is a place of peace
even as on the billowing sea

CODA: 1999-2000

DAVID OLIVEIRA

MILLENNIUM POET LAUREATE

David Oliveira

In 1999, in conjunction with the *Santa Barbara News-Press*, a Millennial Celebration committee was formed, and the members selected David Oliveira as the city's unofficial Poet Laureate. Oliveira read a poem on New Year's Eve at the Santa Barbara Museum of Art, and his poem, along with several others by local poets, was published in the newspaper several days later.

According to Oliveira, "There was talk of going before the city council at the time, but I think after the great millennium night the committee lost its energy." In 2002, Oliveira moved to Phnom Penh, Cambodia, and it wasn't until 2004 that the Santa Barbara City Council adopted the official resolution for the position.

Currently, being chosen Poet Laureate is a fairly elaborate process. First, a fellow citizen nominates a poet who meets the following review criteria:

- a proven history of substantial publication of individual poems and/or books, including at least one work that is not self-published or by a vanity press;
- an established history of activity in the Santa Barbara literary community, i.e., readings, publications, public presentations, and/or teaching;
- and critical acclaim as demonstrated by special honors, awards, or other recognition.

All nominations are then put before the Poet Laureate Review Committee, which makes a recommendation to the Arts Advisory Committee, which in turn makes a recommendation to the City Council and the Mayor.

Although David Oliveira was not chosen through this process, he is a much-admired poet, and his generosity to other Santa Barbara poets is well known. All the poets in this volume are in agreement that the collection would not be complete without a valedictory poem by

Oliveira, and his "The End of the Twentieth Century"—insightful and wise—seems a fitting way to conclude the book.

David Oliveira is the author of *In the Presence of Snakes* (Brandenburg Press) and *A Little Travel Story* (Harbor Mountain Press). His other works include *A Near Country: Poems of Loss*, a collaboration with Glenna Luschei and Jackson Wheeler (Solo Press) and *How Much Earth: the Fresno Poets* (Heyday Books), an anthology which he edited with Christopher Buckley and M. L. Williams. He is also the inventor of *Poet Cards,* a trading card series featuring poets.

Oliveira was publisher and editor of Mille Grazie Press in Santa Barbara, and a founding editor of *Solo*, a national journal of poetry. He was a board member of the Santa Barbara Poetry Festival and founder of the long-running Santa Barbara Poetry Series. Additionally, he is the recipient of an Individual Artist Award in poetry from the Santa Barbara Arts Fund. He continues to lives in Phnom Penh, where he is Professor of English and Writing Center Director at Paññāsāstra University of Cambodia.

The End of the Twentieth Century

These things are never about precision,
centuries and millenniums,
beginnings and ends.
Mostly accidents of history,
when we start counting and what we count.
If we were born with twelve fingers,
or used our toes like the Mayans,
or if Caesar could have waited
a while longer for his taxes,
the numbers would be different today.
We wouldn't need to be in this hurry
to accomplish something momentous.
We could be lost in blissful abandon,
like those persons with a world of time
before a heart attack or cancer
turns their lives over
to the joys of wheat grass and jogging.
With a little different luck,
a little more press attention,
today could be the end of a century
and we would be stuck—no more accomplished,
no more admired than we are now.

We could learn patience from the Chinese,
surviving forty-six centuries already,
one honorable year at a time.
Of course, calendars in China begin at a different place,

and from here it's hard to see
how the added experience helps their years
begin any better than ours.

Whatever we think about the end of the century,
some of us will be here
on the first morning of the twenty-first to start over;
or none of us,
if predictions for the end of the world come true;
or only the righteous, if their prayers are answered;
or all of us, if in the rush to be counted,
we've misunderstood the way things work.

Whatever happens shouldn't matter much.
Not to the earth, or its dead, or its living
who will wake up to all those answers.

Notes and Acknowledgements

The Santa Barbara Poets Laureate would like to thank the editors and publishers of the journals and books where some of these poems previously appeared. They would also like to thank the many Santa Barbara institutions and individuals who requested poetry during their laureateships.

Perie Longo

"Student Poetry Recitation: Santa Barbara Courthouse Mural Room" was written for Longo's investiture as Santa Barbara's second Poet Laureate on March 9, 2007.

"The Way of Santa Barbara" was written in honor of the 225th anniversary of the Presidio, 1782-2007. The epigraph comes from *Santa Barbara Historical Themes and Images* by Jarrell C. Jackman.

"What Women Want" was written for the Nuclear Age Peace Foundation (NAPF) Annual Peace Awards Ceremony, November, 2009, dedicated to "Women for Peace".

"Dedication" is carved into a stone at the Douglas Family Preserve.

Chryss Yost

"Eduardo Recites Keats' 'Ode on a Grecian Urn'" is dedicated to Eduardo Cortez, winner of the 2013 Santa Barbara County Poetry Out Loud poetry recitation competition, and was read for Yost's investiture as fifth Poet Laureate.

"Flow" was written to honor the completion of the Cater Advanced Water Treatment Project and presented on September 23, 2013.

"California Roots" was written for the dedication of the Cota Sycamore at the Santa Barbara Mission for Huell Howser, April 11, 2014.

"Portrait of a Saint with Schwinn and BBQ Sauce" was inspired by Niccolo di Buonaccorso's "Saint Lawrence," displayed at the Santa Barbara Museum of Art.

"Wicked" was inspired by Penelope Stewart's "Daphne" installation at Lotusland.

Sojourner Kincaid Rolle

"Hosanna" was written in honor of Art and Humanities Month - October 2015

"An Ode to the King Palm at Anacapa Street" was written in honor of the 50th Anniversary of Santa Barbara Beautiful.

www.ingramcontent.com/pod-product-compliance
Lightning Source LLC
Chambersburg PA
CBHW020620300426
44113CB00007B/715